IMPOSSIBLE LOVES

Darío Jaramillo is one of Colombia's foremost poets and novelists, widely acclaimed for re-energising the love poem, and winner of his country's National Poetry Prize (2017). He is the recipient of the International Federico García Lorca Prize (2018) for a lifetime contribution to Spanish literature.

Richard Gwyn is the author of *The Vagabond's Breakfast* (Wales Book of the Year, 2012) and *The Blue Tent* (2019). As a translator from Spanish, his anthology *The Other Tiger* (2016) has introduced a new generation of Latin American poets to readers of English.

IMPOSSIBLE
LOVES

DARÍO JARAMILLO

translated by
RICHARD GWYN

CARCANET

First published in Great Britain in 2019 by
Carcanet
Alliance House, 30 Cross Street
Manchester M2 7AQ
www.carcanet.co.uk

A CIP catalogue record for this book is
available from the British Library.
ISBN 978 1 78410 861 8

Book design by Andrew Latimer
Printed in Great Britain by SRP Ltd, Exeter, Devon

The publisher acknowledges financial
assistance from Arts Council England.

CONTENTS

IMPOSSIBLE LOVES

RAZONES DEL AUSENTE

Si alguien les pregunta por él,
díganle que quizá no vuelva nunca o que si regresa
acaso ya nadie reconozca su rostro;
díganle también que no dejó razones para nadie,
que tenía un mensaje secreto, algo importante que decirles
pero que lo ha olvidado.
Díganle que ahora está cayendo, de otro modo y en otra parte del
    mundo,
díganle que todavía no es feliz,
si esto hace feliz a alguno de ellos; díganle también que se fue con el
    corazón vacío y seco
y díganle que eso no importa ni siquiera para la lástima o el perdón
y ni él mismo sufre por eso,
que ya no cree en nada ni en nadie y mucho menos en él mismo,
    que tantas cosas que vio apagaron su mirada y ahora, ciego,
    necesita del tacto,
díganle que alguna vez tuvo un leve rescoldo de fe en Dios, en un
    día de sol,
díganle que hubo palabras que le hicieron creer en el amor
y luego supo que el amor dura lo que dura una palabra.
Díganle que como un globo de aire perforado a tiros,
su alma fue cayendo hasta el infierno que lo vive y que ni siquiera
    está desesperado
y díganle que a veces piensa que esa calma inexorable es su castigo;
díganle que ignora cuál es su pecado
y que la culpa que lo arrastra por el mundo la considera apenas otro
    dato del problema
y díganle que en ciertas noches de insomnio y aun en otras en que
    cree haberlo soñado,
teme que acaso la culpa sea la única parte de sí mismo que le queda
y díganle que en ciertas mañanas llenas de luz

REASONS FOR HIS ABSENCE

If anyone asks after him,
tell them that perhaps he'll never come back, or else
on returning no one will recognise his face;
tell them also that he left no one any reasons,
that he had a secret message, something important to tell them
but he's forgotten what it was.
Tell them that he is falling, in a different way, and in another part
    of the world;
tell them he is still not happy
if this makes some of them happy; tell them also that he left with
    his heart empty and dry
and tell them that this doesn't matter, not even for pity or pardon's
    sake
and that he himself doesn't suffer on this account,
and that now he doesn't believe in anything or anyone, far less in
    himself, that from seeing so many things his eyes failed him, and
    now, blind, he needs touch,
tell them that once, on a sunny day, he had the faint glimmer
    of a faith in God,
tell them that once there were words that made him believe in love
and that later he learned love lasts
as long as it takes to say a word.
Tell them that like a balloon punctured by gunshot,
his soul plunged toward the hell within, and he isn't even in despair
and tell them that sometimes he thinks this inexorable calm
    is his punishment;
tell them that he doesn't know what sin he has committed
and that he considers the blame he drags around the world
    just another aspect of the problem
and tell them that on certain insomniac nights and even on others
    during which he believes he has dreamt it,

y en medio de tardes de piadosa lujuria y también borracho de vino
en noches de lluvia
siente cierta alegría pueril por su inocencia
y díganle que en esas ocasiones dichosas habla a solas.
Díganle que si alguna vez regresa, volverá con dos cerezas en sus ojos
y una planta de moras sembrada en su estómago y una serpiente
enroscada en su cuello.
Y tampoco esperará nada de nadie y se ganará la vida honradamente,
de adivino, leyendo las cartas y celebrando extrañas ceremonias en las
que no creerá
y díganle que se llevó consigo algunas supersticiones, tres fetiches,
ciertas complicidades mal entendidas
y el recuerdo de dos o tres rostros que siempre vuelven a él en la
oscuridad
y nada.

he is afraid that the blame might be the only part of himself
    that is left
and tell them that on certain luminous mornings
and in the middle of afternoons of merciful lust and also on rainy
    nights drunk with wine
he feels a certain puerile joy in his innocence
and tell them that on these blissful occasions he talks to himself.
Tell them that if some day he returns, he will come with two cherries
    for eyes and a blackberry bush seeding in his stomach and a snake
    coiled around his neck.
And nor will he expect anything from anyone and he will earn his
    living honourably,
as a fortune-teller, reading the cards and celebrating strange ceremonies
    in which he will not believe
and tell them that he made off with some superstitions, three fetishes,
    a few misunderstood instances of complicity
and the memory of two or three faces that always come back to him
    in the darkness
and nothing.

EL OFICIO

La poesía, esa batalla de palabras cansadas; nombres de cosas que
    el ruido escamotea;
llegan fieles a reconocer el signo, heráldica donde cada rito tiene su lugar:
allá la cornucopia; el ara, el gerifalte, aquí muy cerca
    una noche y una estrella:
amplia red de sonidos que ocultan este corazón aterido y amargo,
un gajo de uvas verdes, el silencio irrepetible de una calle de mi infancia.
La poesía: este consuelo de bobos sin amor ni esperanza,
borrachos por el ruido del verbo, aturdidos por cosas que significan otras cosas,
sonidos de sonidos.
Prefiero mirar tus cartas que leerlas; de súbito dibujas un beso;
la poesía: esta langosta, esta alharaca, esta otra cosa que no es ella,
la risa de Alejandra, el esplendor de tantos sueños silenciosos,
una forma callada.

THE TRADE

Poetry, that battle of tired words; names for things that the noise whisks away;
believers come to acknowledge the sign, the heraldry in which every ritual
    has its place:
there the cornucopia; the sacred stone, the gyrfalcon, and here, nearby,
    a night and one star:
a wide network of sounds that hide this frozen and bitter heart,
a bunch of green grapes, the unrepeatable silence of a childhood street.
Poetry: this consolation of idiots without love or hope,
drunk on the sound of words, stunned by things that mean other things,
sounds of sounds.
I prefer to look at your letters than read them; all at once you sketch a kiss;
poetry: this lobster, this song and dance, this other thing that it is not,
Alejandra's laughter, the splendour of so many muffled dreams,
a silent form.

PENÚLTIMA BIOGRAFÍA IMAGINARIA

Él vivió tan intensamente los dos o tres instantes que hacen su vida, la vida,
que la memoria había muerto y no tenía posibilidad de recordarlos:
pero un estigma lo ataba a la certeza de que algún modo
aquellos instantes todavía eran suyos;
si me oyera, él no permitiría que les hablara a ustedes de estas cosas,
ni mencionara sus enfermedades más secretas y constantes:
la manía repetida de soñar despierto,
la costumbre de cerrar los ojos para ver mejor,
la soledad sin ahínco,
la culpa que lo rodeaba como un mar viscoso,
la sospecha de la luz entrevista y de que él conservaba algo más antiguo de él
    mismo, que no estaba manchado,
que de algún modo permanecía inocente.
Él vivió tan intensamente los dos o tres instantes que hacen su vida, la vida,
que a fuerza de hacerse querer olvidó que él amaba
y esto lo supo tan bien como para que no le hiciera daño;
y casi siempre parecía viendo llover, aun durante prolongados lapsos
    de sequía
y cuando hablaba parecía hablando el idioma secreto de la lluvia nocturna.
Si me oyera, no me permitiría que les contara a ustedes estas cosas,
aunque es posible que guardara un silencio teñido de vacío,
aunque es posible que abriera los ojos de su sueño
y hablara de animales de fuego y dijera que siente que en su boca está el mar
    de los Sargazos,
aunque es posible que preguntara alelado por algún pasaje remoto de mi vida
y añadiera que nunca hay nada de qué arrepentirse
y luego preguntara ensimismado en qué lugar de la tierra son ahora las tres
    de la mañana,
aunque es posible, acaso, que también sonriera levemente.
En todo caso, él sabría que algo suyo mantendría fluyendo,

PENULTIMATE IMAGINARY BIOGRAPHY

He lived the two or three moments that constitute life, his life, so intensely
that his memory had died and with it the chance to remember them:
but a stigma bound him to the certainty that in some way
those moments were still his;
if he were to hear me, he would not allow me to speak to you of these things,
nor mention his most secret and tenacious ailments:
the recurrent mania for dreaming while awake,
the habit of closing his eyes in order to see better,
the effortless solitude,
the blame that surrounded him like a viscous sea,
the suspicion of glimpsed light, and that he retained some ancient part of
    himself that was not stained,
that in some way remained innocent.
He lived the two or three moments that constitute life, his life, so intensely
that as a result of his efforts to be loved he forgot that he loved
and this he knew well enough for it not to damage him;
and almost always it seemed as though he were watching the rain, even
    during prolonged bouts of drought
and when he spoke, it seemed he was speaking the secret language of the
    rain at night.
If he were to hear me, he would not allow me to speak to you of these things,
although it's possible he would maintain a silence tinged with emptiness,
although it's possible that he would open his eyes from his dream
and speak about creatures of fire and would say that he feels as if inside his
    mouth is the Sargasso Sea,
although it's possible that he would ask, bewildered, for some remote passage
    of my life,
and would add that there is never anything to repent
and later would ask, engrossed, in what place on earth it is now three in the
    morning,

algo suyo que no podría recordar,
dos o tres instantes que tal vez, quien lo sabrá,
todavía no habían llegado.

although it's possible, perhaps, that he would also smile gently.
In any case, he would know that something of his kept flowing,
something of his that he could not remember,
two or three moments that maybe, who can tell,
still had not arrived.

Sobre la geometría del tiempo este poema que recorre
la fría piel de los minutos que ni esperan ni acosan,
sobre la línea de los días sembrados en la metálica luz de los muertos,
florecidos a punta de tanta vida que recorre sus venas de clepsidra.
Sobre el tiempo este poema asomado de reojo a la muerte, sobre el tiempo
hermano de la nada, sobre el tiempo ingrávido gravitando
sobre mi cabeza y sobre la cabeza de mi hermano, sobre el tiempo
este poema, sobre el tiempo que camina por encima de las aguas
y pasa a través de los blancos jardines de yeso de las regiones del norte,
sobre el tiempo olvidado de los juegos de la tortuga y Aquiles,
sobre el tiempo despiadado el asombro impotente del poema,
sobre el silencio que es la música del tiempo terminado y constante y exacto,
teorema de las flores que nacen medidas por el día,
teorema del deseo y la culpa capturados en el largo insomnio
de la noche puntual, de la agorera, lenta noche,
sobre el tiempo inmensurable, midiendo el cambio de piel
de las serpientes, sangrando sobre la sombra del olvido,
sobre el tiempo este monótono poema, sobre el tiempo
que continúa más allá de la vana palabra del poema.

ANOTHER *ARS POÉTICA I*: TIME

Of the geometry of time this poem that runs over
the cold skin of minutes that neither wait nor pester,
of the line of days sown in the metallic light of the dead,
forced to flower by such life as flows in their water-clock veins.
Of time this poem peering sideways at death, of time
brother of nothing, of weightless time gravitating
above my head and above the head of my brother, of time
this poem, of time that walks on water and passes through
the white plaster gardens of the northern regions,
of time forgotten in the games of the tortoise and Achilles,
of ruthless time the impotent astonishment of the poem,
of silence that is the music of time ended and constant and exact,
theorem of flowers whose life is measured by the day,
theorem of desire and blame captured in the long insomnia
of the punctual night, of the slow, ominous night,
of time immeasurable, that measures the shedding
of serpents' skin, bleeding over the shadow of oblivion,
of time this monotonous poem, of time that continues
far beyond the vain words of the poem.

RELATO

Cuando los seres de carne y hueso abandonaron su corazón
    como si la fiebre por una tierra nueva se agotara
pequeñas cosas invadieron su cuerpo y las amplias
    estancias donde habitaba su desaliento;
ella rinde culto a los objetos hermosos, a la copa de
    vino, a la cabeza de barro, a fotos y fetiches,
reliquias para llenar el hueco de lo que pudo haber sido,
    ella busca la tierra incendiada en algún recoveco del olvido,
heridas sobre la piel de la esquizofrenia, ella acumula
    ademanes para aplazar la muerte;
Dama de Fetiche, Curandera, Señora de la Crisma Rota:
ella sobrevive al careo del suicidio, lo atrapa entre
    cristal y porcelana, lo irriga con té helado,
lo perfuma con tabaco rubio, lo invade con el fantasma
    de un calígrafo muerto que la posee
y es el dueño de su insomnio y la arrulla con un
    concierto de piano en la vena aorta;
una flor llamada crisantemo, la sequedad de la carne:
    ideogramas de un calcinado corazón ansioso;
Ama del Sueño Sonámbulo, ella camina por la escalera
    en espiral que lleva al fondo del Caribe;
ella se aferra al fósil de una rosa hace mil años marchita;
    fila de espejos que termina y comienza en Santa Rosa,
de las sillas vienesas a las sillas vienesas, la huella dactilar
    de la locura impresa para siempre sobre el tedio.

STORY

When the beings of flesh and blood fled her heart
    as if the fever for a new world exhausted them
small things invaded her body and the spacious
    rooms where her despondency used to linger;
she worships beautiful objects, the glass
    of wine, the head of clay, photos and fetishes,
relics to fill the vacuum of what might have been,
    she searches the burnt earth in some corner of oblivion,
wounds on the skin of schizophrenia, she accumulates
    gestures to appease death;
Fetish Woman; Healer; Our Lady of the Broken Crown;
she survives the face-off with suicide, traps it between
    glass and porcelain, waters it with iced tea,
perfumes it with blonde tobacco, invades it with the ghost
    of a dead calligrapher who possesses her
and is the owner of her insomnia and lulls her to sleep
    with a piano concerto in the aortic vein;
a flower called chrysanthemum, dryness of the flesh:
    ideograms of a scorched and anxious heart;
Lady of Somnambulant Sleep, she walks down the spiral
    staircase that reaches the floor of the Caribbean;
she clings to the fossil of a rose that withered a thousand years ago;
    a line of mirrors that ends and begins in Santa Rosa,
of bentwood chairs and bentwood chairs, the fingerprint trace
    of madness pressed for ever over the tedium.

VENGANZA

Ahora tú, vuelta poema,
encasillada en versos que te nombran,
la hermosa, la innombrable, luminosa,
ahora tú, vuelta poema,
tu cuerpo, resplandor,
escarcha, desecho de palabra,
poema apenas tu cuerpo
prisionero en el poema,
vuelto versos que se leen en la sala,
tu cuerpo que es pasado
y es este poema
esta pobre venganza.

VENGEANCE

You now, turned into a poem,
pigeon-holed by lines that name you,
the beautiful, the unnameable, luminous,
you now, turned into a poem,
your body, a radiance,
frost, debris of words,
barely a poem your body
imprisoned in the poem,
turned into lines that are read in the drawing room,
your body a thing of the past
and this poem
this feeble vengeance.

ÁLBUM DE FOTOS

Tánger, enero 14 de 1977.
Germán, montado en un camello,
conserva en la foto un hálito
que ya le arrebataron los gusanos.
Ahora él es algo muy hermoso que no existe,
que perdí;
acaso sea el fantasma que me crispa,
el ángel borracho de mis pesadillas escogidas;
también, carajo, un millón antiguo de castillos en el aire.
Tánger, enero 14 de 1977;
la insomne acumulación de noches
no pasa sobre el rostro de la foto;
ahora esto no es más que parte de mi nada:
mi podrido inexistente amigo,
mi suicidada víscera, mi elaborada desmemoria.
Tánger, enero 14 de 1977.
El tiempo detenido, Germán sonriendo
en una foto cada vez más amarilla
y ahora quiero matarlo definitivamente en estos versos
una semana después de que se tomó no sé cuántos Seconales;
la literatura es una lepra:
no me contará cuáles son las delicias secretas de una crisis,
no le diré hasta donde es una virtud la confusión.
Stop. Corten.

PHOTOGRAPH ALBUM

Tangiers, 14th of January, 1977.
Germán, mounted on a camel,
his halo – which by now has been carried off
by worms – is intact in the photo.
He is something beautiful that now does not exist,
that I lost;
perhaps he is the ghost that sets me on edge,
the drunken angel of my selected nightmares;
along with – damn it – those million castles in the air.
Tangiers, 14th of January, 1977;
the insomniac build-up of nights
leaves no mark on the face in the photo;
this is now nothing more than a part of my nothingness:
my rotting non-existent friend,
my suicided viscera, my intricate misremembering.
Tangiers, 14th of January, 1977.
Time stopped, Germán smiling
in an ever-yellowing photo
and now I want to kill him off once and for all in these lines
a week after he took I don't know how many Seconal;
literature is a scourge:
he won't tell me what the secret delights of a crisis are,
and I won't tell him to what extent confusion is a virtue.
Stop. Cut.

JOB OTRA VEZ

Hábito o virtud, monótona paciencia que aprendo con dolor,
día por día, lentamente.
Vicio o costumbre que se adquiere contra las ansias,
paciencia que me elude con el ruido,
agridulce paciencia que no necesito cuando llega la dicha
o cuando vibro con el ritmo del tiempo
y la serenidad consiste en vivir como quien sabe inútil
    todo forcejeo,
que todo llega si está escrito que llegue,
que no hemos escogido ser luz o tiniebla.
Diosa paciencia que gobierna los trenes retrasados
y prescribe los rigores del nubarrón a los bañistas,
virtud profesional del chofer y el relojero,
virtud amarga para los malos tiempos,
seca virtud sin lírica y sin ángel,
invisible rectora de las leyes del turno,
paciencia que aprendo sin aprenderla nunca,
paciencia que aparece en el poema para recordarme que ya
    no soy tan joven,
que esta vida se acaba.
Virtud de sangre fría, flor de hielo,
agria destilación del alma para acercarnos a la muerte.

JOB AGAIN

Habit or virtue, monotonous patience that I learn painfully,
slowly, day by day.
Vice or custom that is acquired against anxiety,
patience which eludes me in all the noise,
bittersweet patience that I don't need when I'm happy
or when I buzz with the rhythm of time
and serenity consists in living like one who knows how useless is
 all struggle,
that everything will come if it is written that it will come,
that we haven't chosen to be light or darkness.
Goddess patience who governs the lateness of trains
and prescribes the severity of a storm cloud for swimmers,
professional virtue of the chauffeur and the clockmaker,
bitter virtue for bad times,
dry virtue without song and without angels,
invisible dean of the laws of the moment,
patience that I learn nothing by learning,
patience that appears in the poem to remind me that I am
 no longer young,
that this life ends.
Virtue of cold blood, flower of ice,
bitter brew of the soul to accustom us to death.

Recuerdo solamente que he olvidado el acento de las
    más amadas voces,
y que perdí para siempre el olor de las frutas de la infancia,
el sabor exacto del durazno,
el aleteo del aire frío entre los pinos,
el entusiasmo al descubrir una nuez que ha caído del nogal.
Sortilegios de otro día que ahora son apenas letanía incolora,
vana convocatoria que no me trae el asombro de ver un
    colibrí entre mi cuarto,
como muchas madrugadas de mi infancia.
¿Cómo recuperar ciertas caricias y los más esenciales abrazos?
¿Cómo revivir la más cierta penumbra, iluminada apenas
    con la luz de los Beatles,
y cómo hacer que llueva la misma lluvia que veía caer
    a los trece años?
¿Cómo tornar al éxtasis de sol, a la luz ebria de mis siete años,
al sabor maduro de la mora,
a todo aquel territorio desconocido por la muerte,
a esa palpitante luz de la pureza,
a todo esto que soy yo y que ya no es mío?

I remember only that I've forgotten the accent of the voices
    I most loved,
and that I've lost for ever the smell of the fruits of my childhood,
the precise taste of peach,
the flurry of cold air between the pines,
the excitement of discovering a walnut fallen from its tree.
Enchantments from the past that are now just a colourless refrain,
a vain summons when the astonishment of seeing a hummingbird
    inside my bedroom – as on many mornings of my childhood –
brings me no wonder.
How to recover certain caresses and dearest embraces?
How to re-live the perfect half-light, barely illuminated by the glow
    of The Beatles,
and how to make it rain the way it rained when I was thirteen?
How to return to the ecstasy of the sun, to the intoxicated light
    of seven years old,
to the ripe taste of blackberry,
to all that territory unvisited by death,
to that pulsing light of innocence,
to all that I am and that is no longer mine?

DE LA NOSTALGIA, 3

Diluir la memoria en una especie de estupor anhelante,
picaflor sin urgencias que enumera los lugares más tibios,
alelada memoria,
la muy frío espejo de calor de otro entonces,
memoria que pregunta cuánta materia de mi cuerpo queda
de aquellos cuerpos míos que vivieron cada alucinación
    y cada asombro,
cada cosa que hoy es nada,
y aún menos que nada,
si es palabra.

NOSTALGIA, 3

To dilute memory in a kind of wistful stupor,
unhurried hummingbird who lists the warmest places,
bewildered memory,
cold mirror of another time's heat,
memory that asks how much of my bodily matter remains
from those of my bodies that experienced each hallucination
    and each bewilderment,
each and every thing that now is nothing,
and even less than nothing
if a word.

DE LA NOSTALGIA, 5

Alelado bajo el sol, sobre la tapia,
soy un niño de cinco años narcotizado por la luz,
suspendido fuera del tiempo,
del tiempo que ahora es cosa ajena, intermitencia del paisaje,
sustancia del lejano horizonte de montañas azules.
Descubro un éxtasis perfecto, matutino,
hago parte del aire, soy brisa inaugural, soy ala y vuelo,
dejo de ser yo mismo felizmente fundido con la luz,
nazco y regreso.

NOSTALGIA, 5

Stupefied under the sun, on the garden wall,
I am a child of five, drugged by the light,
suspended outside of time,
of time that is now a thing apart, a flickering of the landscape,
a substance on the far horizon of blue mountains.
I discover perfect morning ecstasy,
I make up a part of the air, I am the unblemished breeze, I am wing
    and flight,
I happily forget myself, melting with the light,
I am born and I return.

DE LA NOSTALGIA, 6

Es distinto este decir que aquel hechizo,
me repito enredado en la guerra de encontrar las palabras.
Ayer iluminación, hoy trampa, evasivo poema,
rescoldo apenas del vuelo del amor o el asombro,
huella penosa de las noches felices,
juego el poema de la luna conmigo, en la noche de ahora.
Está además el vano consuelo de mi desmemoria: que
    conozco la dicha.
Y está también la certeza más sabia y más inútil: que
    hay alguien dentro de mí perdido,
que envejezco.

NOSTALGIA, 6

This saying is different from that magic spell,
I repeat to myself, enmeshed in the war of finding words.
Yesterday illumination, today a snare, evasive poem,
barely an ember of the flight from love or astonishment,
painful trail of happy nights,
I play the moon poem with myself, in the night of now.
There is, what's more, the vain comfort of my forgetfulness:
    that I know joy.
And there is also the wiser and more useless certainty: that
    there is someone inside me, lost,
that I am growing old.

I

Ese otro que también me habita,
acaso propietario, invasor quizás o exiliado en este cuerpo ajeno
    o de ambos,
ese otro a quien temo e ignoro, felino o ángel,
ese otro que está solo siempre que estoy solo, ave o demonio,
esa sombra de piedra que ha crecido en mi adentro y en mi
    afuera,
eco o palabra, esa voz que responde cuando me preguntan algo,
el dueño de mi embrollo, el pesimista y el melancólico y el
    inmotivadamente alegre,
ese otro,
también te ama.

LOVE POEMS

I

That other who also lives in me,
the owner perhaps, or a squatter or exile in this body
　　that is alien or else both of ours,
that other whom I fear and ignore, feline or angel,
that other who is always alone when I am alone, bird or demon,
　　that shadow of a rock that has grown inside me and outside me,
echo or word, that voice that answers when something is asked of me,
the master of my confusion, the pessimist and the melancholic and the one
　　who is unreasonably cheerful,
that other,
also loves you.

3

Yo huelo a ti.
Me persigue tu olor, me persigue y me posee.
No es este olor un perfume sobrepuesto sobre ti,
no es el aroma que llevas como una prenda más:
es tu olor más esencial, tu halo único.
Y cuando, ausente, mi vacío te convoca,
una ráfaga de ese aliento me llega del lugar más tierno de la noche.
Yo huelo a ti
y tu olor me impregna después de estar juntos en el lecho,
y ese fino aroma esencial me sustituye.
Yo huelo a ti.

3

I smell of you.
Your smell pursues me, it pursues and possesses me.
This is not a perfume that you put on yourself,
nor is it the scent that you wear like another layer of clothing:
it's your most essential smell, your unique halo.
And when, absent, my emptiness summons you,
a gust of that breath reaches me from the night's most tender place.
I smell of you
and your smell saturates me after we lie together,
and that fine essential aroma replaces me.
I smell of you.

4

Algún día te escribiré un poema que no mencione el aire ni
   la noche;
un poema que omita los nombres de las flores, que no tenga
   jazmines o magnolias.
Algún día te escribiré un poema sin pájaros ni fuentes, un poema
   que eluda el mar
y que no mire a las estrellas.
Algún día te escribiré un poema que se limite a pasar los dedos
   por tu piel
y que se convierta en palabras tu mirada.
Sin comparaciones, sin metáforas, algún día escribiré un poema
   que huela a ti,
un poema con el ritmo de tus pulsaciones, con la intensidad
   estrujada de tu abrazo.
Algún día te escribiré un poema, el canto de mi dicha.

4

One day I will write you a poem that does not mention the air or
    the night;
a poem that omits the names of flowers, that contains no jasmines
    or magnolias.
One day I will write you a poem without birds or fountains, a poem
    that neglects to mention the sea
and that doesn't look at the stars.
One day I will write you a poem that is content to pass its fingers over
    your skin
and that turns your gaze into words.
Without comparisons, without metaphors, one day I will write a poem
that smells of you,
a poem with the rhythm of your pulse, with the intimate intensity
of your embrace.
One day I will write you a poem, the song of my joy.

6

Tu voz por el teléfono tan cerca y nosotros tan distantes,
tu voz, amor, al otro lado de la línea y yo aquí solo, sin ti,
    al otro lado de la luna,
tu voz por el teléfono tan cerca, apaciguándome, and tan lejos
    tú de mí, tan lejos,
tu voz que repasa las tareas conjuntas,
o que menciona un número mágico,
que por encima de la alharaca del mundo me habla para decir
    en lenguaje cifrado que me amas.
Tu voz aquí, a lo lejos, que le da sentido a todo,
tu voz que es la música de mi alma,
tu voz, sonido del agua, conjuro, encantamiento.

6

Your voice on the phone so near and us so distant,
your voice, my love, at the other end of the line and me here alone,
    without you, on the other side of the moon,
your voice on the phone so near, placating me, and you so far from me,
    so far,
your voice that lists the things we must do together,
or mentioning a magic number,
that above the fuss and bustle of the world tells me in coded
    language that you love me.
Your voice here, far away, that gives everything a meaning,
your voice that is my soul's music,
your voice, its sound like water, a charm, a spell.

8

Tu lengua, tu sabia lengua que inventa mi piel,
tu lengua de fuego que me incendia,
tu lengua que crea el instante de demencia, el delirio del
    cuerpo enamorado,
tu lengua, látigo sagrado, brasa dulce,
invocación de los incendios que me saca de mí, que me transforma,
tu lengua de carne sin pudores,
tu lengua de entrega que me demanda todo, tu muy mía lengua,
tu bella lengua que electriza mis labios, que vuelve tuyo mi
    cuerpo por ti purificado,
tu lengua que me explora y me descubre,
tu hermosa lengua que también sabe decir que me ama.

8

Your tongue, your wise tongue that invents my skin,
your fiery tongue that sets me alight,
your tongue that contrives the instant of derangement, delirium
    of the beloved body,
your tongue, sacred whip, sweet ember,
invocation of the fire that empties me out, that transforms me,
your shameless, fleshy tongue,
your compliant tongue that demands all, your tongue so very mine,
your lovely tongue that electrifies my lips, that renders my body yours,
    purified by you,
your tongue that explores me, discovers me,
your beautiful tongue that knows also how to speak its love for me.

Primero está la soledad.

En las entrañas y en el centro del alma:

ésta es la esencia, el dato básico, la única certeza;

que solamente tu respiración te acompaña,

que siempre bailarás con tu sombra,

que esa tiniebla eres tú.

Tu corazón, ese fruto perplejo, no tiene que agriarse con tu
  sino solitario;

déjalo esperar sin esperanza

que el amor es un regalo que algún día llega por sí solo.

Pero primero está la soledad,

y tú estás solo,

tú estás solo con tu pecado original – contigo mismo –.

Acaso una noche, a las nueve,

aparece el amor y todo estalla y algo se ilumina dentro de ti,

y te vuelve otro, menos amargo, más dichoso;

pero no olvides, especialmente entonces,

cuando llegue el amor y te calcine,

que primero y siempre está tu soledad

y luego nada

y después, si ha de llegar, está el amor.

13

First there is solitude.
In the guts and at the centre of the soul:
this is the essence, the basic data, the only certainty:
that only your breathing accompanies you,
that you will always dance with your shadow,
that the darkness is you.
Your heart, that troubled fruit, need not grow bitter with your
    solitary fate:
let it wait without hope
that love is a gift which one day shows up of its own accord.
But first there is solitude,
and you are alone
you are alone with your original sin – with you own self.
Maybe one night, at nine o'clock,
love appears and everything explodes and something lights up inside you,
and you become someone else, less bitter, more joyous;
but don't forget, above all then,
when love arrives and scorches you
that first and always is your solitude
and later nothing
and afterwards, if it should arrive, there is love.

PLATÓN BORRACHO

He habitado la más absoluta claridad:
la luz es la precisa para alumbrar el perfil exacto de las cosas,
la sombra forma parte de la luz, ayuda a ver:
este árbol corresponde al arquetipo que recuerdo,
todo se ajusta con la idea,
este pétalo es el pétalo eterno
y será mañana el eterno pétalo marchito;
por un instante tengo lucidez absoluta, pero ya no soy ese que
    escribió la primera palabra de este verso;
la charada está incompleta y no logro descifrar la clave del embrollo;
sé lo más fácil:
que este caballo que galopa por la playa, majestuosamente ha galopado
    desde siempre en otra playa,
sé que el amor es completarse,
sé mi desdicha y mi ignorancia, que el tiempo nos contiene
    y no lo vemos,
y sé que en otro mundo hay otro, que reflejo, más borracho que yo,
    más ignorante y desdichado.

PLATO, DRUNK

I have experienced absolute clarity:
the light is perfect to bring out the precise profile of things,
shadow makes up an element of light, helps us to see:
this tree corresponds to the archetype I remember,
everything adjusts to the idea,
this petal is the eternal petal
and tomorrow will be the eternal withered petal;
for an instant I possess absolute lucidity, but I am no longer the one
    who wrote the first word of this poem;
the charade is incomplete and I am unable to unravel this mess;
I know what is easiest:
that this horse which gallops along the beach has galloped majestically
    on another beach forever,
I know that to love is to complete oneself,
I know I am wretched and ignorant, that time contains us and we
    do not see it,
and I know that in another world there is another, whom I reflect,
    drunker than me, more wretched and more ignorant.

Mi hermano tiene la línea de la vida corta y marcada intensamente,
una señal profunda, como si una estrella de fuego le hubiera horadado
   la mano y el rumbo.
Mi hermano sabe decir que no con la dureza y la suavidad de los
   hombres vigorosos.
Mi hermano le ha enseñado a su cuerpo la alucinación y el éxtasis,
ha cantado y reído, mi hermano ha vivido siempre como un sabio,
pisando el límite exacto de la demencia, tocando su borde alucinado,
en la fiebre del hongo o el alcohol, en el delirio del amor o de la orgía.
Pero siempre mi hermano ha sido fuerte y sabio,
con la sabiduría de quien sabe el límite de su destrucción
y con la sabiduría de quien se conserva intacto,
mi hermano juega con el tiempo, yuxtapone colores,
mi hermoso quinto hermano me enseña con su historia el fondo
   transparente de su calma
y me extiende la misma mano que quemó todas sus naves
jugándose el todo por el todo, siempre,
y siempre incólume
como quien sabe el final y no le duele.
Mi hermano, el sabio transgresor, regresándome a la ebriedad y al
   incesto,
el furiosamente libre, el desatado de toda obligación que no sea su
   instinto.
Mi quinto hermano es duro y seco con la gente, intolerante como yo,
pero mucho más recio, como quien está acostumbrado a guardar su
   territorio de invasiones.
Mi hermano regala una cálida ternura a quienes ama,
y entonces es locuaz y regocijante y más hermoso.
Mi hermano habla poco
y en ciertos momentos de lucidez alcohólica me dijo que él nunca
   moriría, que algún día se irá,

TESTIMONY CONCERNING MY BROTHER

My brother has a short and deeply furrowed life-line,
a profound sign, as if a shooting star had pierced his hand and his path.
My brother knows how to say no firmly and smoothly like all strong men.
My brother has taught his body hallucination and ecstasy,
has sung and laughed; my brother has always lived like a sage,
pacing the exact limits of insanity, touching its deluded edge,
in mushroom or alcohol fever, in the delirium of love or orgy.
But my brother has always been strong and wise,
with the wisdom of one who knows the limits of his self-destruction
and with the wisdom of one who keeps himself intact,
my brother plays with time, juxtaposes colours,
my beautiful fifth brother teaches me with his story the transparent
    depths of his calm
and offers me the same hand that burned all his boats
always playing for all and everything,
and always unharmed
like one who knows the end but it does not hurt him.
My brother, the wise transgressor, furiously free, unchained from all
    obligation except to his instinct,
returning me to drunkenness and incest.
My fifth brother is hard and dry with people, intolerant like me,
but much tougher, like one who is used to securing his territory from
    invaders.
My brother bestows a warm affection on those he loves,
and then is talkative and cheerful and more beautiful.
My brother talks little
and at given moments of alcoholic lucidity has told me he would never
    die, that one day he will leave,
perhaps disappear,
but that we will always be together, in some way,
as always.

que a lo mejor desaparezca,
pero que siempre estaremos juntos, de algún modo,
como siempre.
Debimos conocernos cuatro años antes, también me dijo mi hermano en esa noche,
pero yo creo que todo tiene su día, su destiempo,
su oscura constelación de alborozado abrazo.
Desde muy joven, sabiendo lo que hacía,
mi quinto hermano quemó todas sus naves,
y abrió los ojos y descubrió su hermoso cuerpo
y supo también que la belleza es la sabiduría del cuerpo
y siempre estuvo atento, creciendo hacia dentro en afiebrada vigilia.
Mi hermano fabrica conmigo fantasías de diecisiete pisos, con risas y palabras,
mi hermano hace música y dice disparates y le gusta echar mentiras que no le hacen
    daño a nadie,
y le fascinan los perfumes y hacer ejercicio y quemarse bajo el sol
y le gusta estar solo, organizando los oficios diarios.
Mi quinto hermano es fuerte y sabio
y ambos sabemos que nunca nosotros, solitarios, dejaremos de estar juntos.
Falta también aquí el sabor amargo que vela tras la sombra de mi quinto hermano,
la pesadilla y el descenso a los infiernos:
él siempre se jugó el todo por el todo
y desaparecerá en la plenitud,
cuando el agrio fantasma que lo sigue sin tocarlo, decida por él,
y caiga,
y con él caiga lo que quede de mí,
si entonces algo queda.

We should have met four years earlier, my brother told me that night too,
but I think that everything has its day, its bad timing,
its dark constellation of jubilant embrace.
From a young age, knowing what he was about,
my fifth brother burned all his boats,
and opened his eyes and discovered his beautiful body
and knew also that beauty is the wisdom of the body,
and he was ever alert, growing inward in a feverish wakefulness.
My brother and I invent fantasies of seventeen storeys, with laughter and
    words,
my brother makes music and talks nonsense and likes to tell lies that don't
    harm anyone,
and is captivated by perfumes and working out and burning in the sun
and he likes to be alone, going about his daily tasks.
My fifth brother is strong and wise
and we both know that the two of us, loners, will never be apart.
The sour taste that keeps vigil over my fifth brother's shadow is also
    missing here,
the nightmare and the descent to hell:
he always played for all or nothing
and will disappear in his prime,
when the bitter ghost that follows without touching him, decides for him,
and he falls,
and with him falls what is left of me,
if, by then, anything is left.

2. PIEDRA

Nube sólida,
más antiguo habitante del planeta,
llama congelada,
debajo de una piedra mi cadáver,
encima de la piedra el río,
la huella del viajero,
piedra o Dios, piedra eterna,
materia de tan inerte, viva,
materia material, materia cataléptica,
continente y contenido,
voluta que el agua deja asir,
piedra abuela, silenciosa,
silenciosa, quieta.

WHEN WE SAY STONE, WE SAY NOTHING

2. STONE

Solid cloud,
most ancient resident of the planet,
frozen flame,
under a stone my corpse,
above the stone the river,
traveller's trace,
stone or God, eternal stone,
matter so inert, alive,
material matter, cataleptic matter,
continent and contents,
scroll that nature leaves rolled up,
grandmother stone, silent,
silent, calm.

10. VIRTUDES DE LA PIEDRA

Paciente, la piedra deja que le penetre el musgo y se deleita
　　sintiendo cómo el sol quema el musgo y la calienta.
Tímida, el contacto con el agua le cambia el color.
Religiosa, la inmovilidad es evidencia de que la piedra
　　es budista.
Justa, cumple con celo la ley de gravitación universal.
Eterna, la piedra es anterior a las pirámides, que son de piedra.
Profundas, el piso del océano es de piedra.
Bella, la piedra es bella como la piedra.
Discreta, la piedra nunca contará nada.
Díscola, lanzada por David, siempre buscará la cabeza de Goliath.
Original, ninguna piedra se parece a otra piedra.
Santas, en el infierno no hay piedras. Por eso el infierno
　　está empedrado de buenas intenciones.
Condenada, la piedra que peque se ata a un hombre escandaloso
　　y se arroja al fondo del mar.

10. VIRTUES OF STONE

Patient, stone allows the moss to settle and delights in feeling the sun's warmth as its scorches the moss.

Shy, contact with water changes its colour.

Religious, immobility is evidence that stone is Buddhist.

Fair, it zealously fulfils the law of universal gravitation.

Eternal, stone came before the pyramids, which are made of stone.

Deep, the floor of the ocean is stone.

Beautiful, stone is as beautiful as stone.

Discreet, stone will never tell anything.

Defiant, cast by David, it will always find Goliath's head.

Original, no stone resembles any other stone.

Holy, in hell there are no stones. That is why the road to hell is paved with good intentions.

Condemned, the stone that sins attaches itself to a scandalous man and hurls itself to the bottom of the sea.

AMORES IMPOSIBLES

2

Un amor imposible es el más feliz de los amores.
O puede serlo.
Basta que nunca creas que es posible un amor imposible
y esto hará la felicidad del amor imposible.
Puede que seas el amor imposible de tu amor imposible.
Pero esto es un milagro.

4

La música sostiene los amores imposibles,
los alimenta con la presencia etérea de una canción,
una canción que es la nuestra aunque sólo la oiga solo.
El amor imposible guarda equilibrio perfecto
sobre la cuerda de una guitarra,
se embriaga con la dulce nostalgia de una polonesa,
se estremece con una voz entre gemido y canto.
Entonces el amor imposible se convierte en guitarra, en piano,
o es el sonido de una voz.
La música es el tiempo presente de los amores imposibles.

IMPOSSIBLE LOVES

2

Impossible love is the happiest of loves.
Or can be.
The only way to find happiness in impossible love
is never to believe impossible love is possible.
You could just be the impossible love of your impossible love.
But that would be a miracle.

4

Music sustains impossible loves,
nurtures them with the ethereal presence of a song,
a song that is ours even though I listen to it only when alone.
Impossible love allows a guitar string
perfect equilibrium,
gets drunk on the sweet nostalgia of a polonaise,
quivers with a voice between a moan and a song.
Then impossible love becomes a guitar, a piano
or is the sound of a voice.
Music is the present tense of impossible loves.

16

Yo no voy nunca solo al fondo de mí mismo.
Jules Supervielle

Yo no voy nunca solo al fondo de mí mismo,
me acompañan mis amores imposibles
– los amores posibles no me amarían
si conocieran el fondo de mí mismo–,
allá voy con mis amores imposibles,
con ellos exorcizo los demonios que habitan
el fondo de mí mismo.
Mis amores imposibles me llevan de la mano en mi trastienda,
conocen las miserias más secretas del fondo de mí mismo,
me ayudan a domesticar mis fieras interiores
me consuelan,
me apaciguan.

18

Yo fui lentamente a tumbos perdiéndome.
Damián Bayón

Yo fui lentamente a tumbos perdiéndome
sin rumbo y contra las paredes,
yo me aniquilé por capricho de un mal amor posible.
Sufrí. Descendí a los infiernos, a varios infiernos,
usé las máscaras más degradantes, repté.
Sufrí.
Vinieron a salvarme los amores imposibles,
Amores sin astucia y sin heridas,
amores curativos que no existen.

16

I never visit my deepest self alone.
Jules Supervielle

I never visit my deepest self alone.
my impossible loves come with me
– possible loves would not love me
if they knew my deepest self –
I go there with my impossible loves,
with them I exorcise the demons that live
within my deepest self.
My impossible loves lead me by the hand in my backroom,
they know the most secret sorrows of my deepest self,
they help me tame the beast within
they console me,
they soothe me.

18

I stumbled along slowly and was lost.
Damián Bayón

I stumbled along slowly and was lost –
aimless and out of my mind,
I destroyed myself on the whim of a bad possible love.
I suffered. I went to hell, to several hells,
I used the most degrading masks, I grovelled.
I suffered.
Impossible loves came to save me,
loves without guile and without wounds,
healing loves that do not exist.

DESOLLAMIENTOS

… the seafaring man with one leg….
R.L. *Stevenson*

Sin pie mi cuerpo sigue amando lo mismo
y mi alma se sale al lugar que ya no ocupo,
fuera de mí:
no, no hay aquí símbolos,
el cuerpo se acomoda a la pasión
y la pasión al cuerpo que pierde sus fragmentos
y continua integro, sin misterios, incólume.
Contra la muerte tengo la mirada y la risa,
soy dueño del abrazo de mi amigo
y del latido sordo de un corazón ansioso.
Contra la muerte tengo el dolor en el pie que no tengo,
un dolor tan real como la muerte misma
y unas ganas enormes de caricias, de besos,
de saber el nombre propio de un árbol que me obsede,
de aspirar un perdido perfume que persigo,
de oír ciertas canciones que recuerdo a fragmentos,
de acariciar mi perro,
de que timbre el teléfono a las seis de la mañana,
de seguir este juego.

FLAYINGS

... the seafaring man with one leg....
R.L. Stevenson

With only one foot my body carries on loving just the same
and my soul goes to the place that I no longer occupy,
outside of me:
no, here there are no symbols,
the body adapts itself to passion
and passion to the body that loses its parts
and continues intact, without mysteries, unharmed.
In the face of death I have my way of looking and my laughter,
I am the owner of my friend's embrace
and of the muffled beat of an eager heart.
In the face of death I have a pain in my missing foot,
a pain as real as death itself
and a huge desire for caresses, kisses,
for knowing the correct name for a tree that obsesses me,
for breathing in a lost scent that I pursue,
for certain songs I remember in fragments,
for the pleasure of stroking my dog,
for the phone to ring at six in the morning,
for this game to carry on.

MOZART EN LA AUTOPISTA

Cierro la ventana,
alejo los zumbidos de otros autos
y voy en mi cápsula a ochenta kilómetros por hora,
entre Mozart,
donde tiempo y espacio, horas y kilómetros no cuentan
y un clarinete puede ser la causa primera,
la explicación de todo,
la punta del ovillo.
Mozart en la autopista.
El mundo es claro y feliz.

MOZART ON THE MOTORWAY

I close the window,
ward off the din of other cars
and go along in my capsule at eighty kilometres an hour,
with Mozart,
where time and space, hours and kilometres don't count
and a clarinet might be the prime cause,
the explanation of everything,
the heart of the matter.
Mozart on the motorway.
The world is bright and happy.

GATOS

I

La luna dora los techos.
Inesperadas, aparecen las sombras de los gatos.
Son tan sigilosos
que son solamente sus sombras.
Ellos ven todo sin ser vistos
y todo debe estar quieto mientras se mueven
para que ellos puedan sentirse inmóviles,
los gatos, sus sombras.

2

Nube en forma de gato:
gato que come lunas,
sigiloso carnívoro del cielo,
disfrazado de nube
o embozado en lo oscuro,
gato que devora estrellas.
Agazapado, vigila las órbitas
y las engulle en la noche,
gato que come lunas.

CATS

1

The moon gilds the rooftops.
Unannounced, the shadows of cats appear.
They are so stealthy
they are only their shadows.
They see everything without being seen
and everything must be still while they move
so they can feel themselves to be unmoving,
the cats, their shadows.

2

Cloud in the shape of a cat:
cat that eats moons.
stealthy carnivore of the sky,
disguised as a cloud
or muffled in the darkness,
cat that devours stars.
Crouching, it surveys the heavenly spheres
and guzzles them in the night,
cat that eats moons.

3

Estados de la materia.
Los estados de la materia son cuatro:
líquido, sólido, gaseoso y gato.
El gato es un estado especial de la materia,
si bien caben las dudas:
¿es materia esta voluptuosa contorsión?
¿no viene del cielo esta manera de dormir?
Y este silencio, ¿acaso no procede de un lugar sin tiempo?
Cuando el espíritu juega a ser materia
entonces se convierte en gato.

4

No son de este mundo,
los gatos no son de este mundo,
pasan de puntillas,
observan en la oscuridad,
espían para Dios o el diablo,
hacen pereza aburridos de este mundo,
los gatos: invasores, testigos.

3

States of matter.
The states of matter are four in number:
liquid, solid, gaseous and cat.
The cat is a special state of matter
although doubts remain:
Is this voluptuous contortion matter?
Is this way of sleeping not heaven-sent?
And this silence: might it emerge from a place without time?
When spirit plays at being matter
it turns into cat.

4

They are not of this world,
cats are not of this world,
they pass by on tiptoe,
they watch in the darkness,
they spy for God or the devil,
they are idlers, bored by this world,
cats: squatters, witnesses.

5

Aletargados en perpetua siesta
después de inconfesables andanzas nocturnas,
desentendidos o alertas,
los gatos están en la casa para ser consentidos,
para dejarse amar indiferentes.
Dios hizo los gatos para que hombres y mujeres
    aprendan a estar solos.

6

Sabiduría del gato:
hacer pereza todo el día sin llegar nunca al tedio.
Materialización del gato:
cuando el gato se convierte en materia, saca las uñas.
Astucia del gato:
fingir que es un animal doméstico.
Silencio del gato:
los gatos guardan todos los secretos de la noche.
Misterios del gato:
todo en el gato es misterioso.

5

Lethargic in perpetual siesta
after unspeakable midnight wanderings,
detached or alert,
cats are in the house to be spoiled:
indifferent, they allow themselves to be loved.
God made cats so that men and women could learn
    to be alone.

6

Wisdom of the cat:
To be idle all day without ever being bored.
Materialisation of the cat:
when the cat becomes matter, it extends its claws.
Guile of the cat:
it pretends to be a domestic animal.
Silence of the cat:
cats keep all the secrets of the night.
Mysteries of the cat:
everything about the cat is mysterious.

10

A oscuras o con luz,
el gato distingue todos los objetos
con insoportable claridad.
También dormido,
el gato ve con nitidez la imagen de sus sueños.
Para librarlo de las torturas de la buena vista
Dios le dio al gato
la indiferencia.

15

Casi todos los gatos
son gatos.
Pero existen gatos que no son gatos.
Que los hay los hay:
se sabe de brujas que se meten entre un gato
y nadie cuenta de gatos convertidos en bruja.
Puede ocurrir que un gato sea tan indolente
que deje de ser gato sin volverse nada distinto,
sólo un gato tan perezoso
que le da pereza ser gato.

10

In darkness or in light
the cat makes out all objects
with unbearable clarity.
While asleep, too,
the cat sees in fine detail the images of its dreams.
To free it from the torment of clear sight
God gave the cat
indifference.

15

Nearly all cats
are cats.
But there are also cats that are not cats.
There are, to be sure:
we know about witches who take the form of a cat
and no one speaks of cats who turn into witches.
It could happen that a cat is so laid back
that it ceases to be a cat without becoming anything else,
a cat so idle
that it can't be bothered with being a cat.

19

Unos encarnan a Dios en un gato y profesan el gateísmo.
Otros creen que cada gato es un Dios y son gatólatras.
Unos y otros ven un lado de la misma moneda.
Todos ignoran que Dios duerme la siesta
desde toda la eternidad
y que los gatos de esta tierra
son dioses mientras duermen.

20

Los gatos no lloran.
Los gatos no tienen motivos ni tampoco lágrimas.
En cambio saben reír casi en silencio.
Ciertos ronroneos profundos son su risa mas sonora.
Casi siempre los gatos están riendo.
Hacia adentro ríen los gatos
sin mostrar demasiada euforia
y sin contarle a nadie que el mundo es gracioso a los ojos
    del gato.
Cuando bostezan los gatos le sonríen al sueño.
Mientras duermen conversan con los ángeles,
en silencio conversan ángeles y gatos sin saber quiénes
    son cuáles,
poseídos de placidez.
Los gatos no lloran.

19

Some embody God in a cat's form and profess Catism.
Others believe that every cat is a God and are Catolators.
They represent two sides of the same coin.
All of them overlook the fact that God has taken a siesta
for all eternity
and that the cats of this world
are gods while they sleep.

20

Cats don't cry.
Cats have no cause to cry, nor tears.
However, they know how to laugh in almost silence.
Some of their purring is the most sonorous laughter.
Cats are almost always laughing.
Cats laugh on the inside
without displaying too much euphoria
and without telling anyone the world is amusing
    in the eyes of a cat.
When they yawn, cats are smiling at the prospect of sleep.
While they sleep, they converse with angels;
they chat in silence, cat and angels, without knowing
    which are which,
settled in repose.
Cats don't cry.

Palabras para hablar de los gatos:
No hay palabras para hablar de los gatos.
Los palabras no abarcan a los gatos.
Los gatos son indiferentes
con los seres que hablan.
Un ladrido puede molestarlos
y un estruendo asusta a los gatos.
Pero los gatos no oyen las palabras.
no les interesa nada que pueda decirse con palabras.
¿Para qué las palabras si hay olfato,
para qué las palabras
si es posible el silencio?

Words for speaking about cats:
there are no words for speaking about cats.
Words do not encompass cats.
Cats are indifferent
to beings who speak.
A bark might disturb them
and a thunder-clap give cats a shock.
But cats do not hear words,
they are not interested in anything that can be said with words.
Why words when you can have smell?
Why words when
silence is possible?

CAUCHO

El árbol de caucho es líquido,
sus hojas son agua, agua verde que respira,
surtidor detenido.
A su sombra, la tierra nunca está seca
y su tronco es humedad hecha madera.
Porción de selva en mi jardín,
árbol esponja, árbol laguna,
pulsación de los ríos subterráneos,
el verde caucho
viene de las profundidades del mar,
en el caucho no se separaron las aguas de la tierra
desde el primer día de la creación.

RUBBER TREE

The rubber tree is liquid,
its leaves are water, green breathing water,
motionless provider.
In its shade, the earth is never dry
and its trunk is humidity become wood.
A piece of forest in my garden,
sponge tree, lake tree,
pulsing of subterranean rivers,
green rubber
comes from the depths of the sea,
in the rubber tree water and earth have not divided
since the first day of creation.

SABOR

Fibras enredadas entre la dentadura,
dulzor definitivo,
azúcar que es agua, agua que es azúcar,
jugo entre hilos,
pequeño planeta entre rojo y amarillo,
fruta que se desprende segregando una goma,
fruta amarilla que se sonroja
disculpándose de su propia perfección.
El mango es una prueba
de la existencia de Dios.

TASTE

Fibres tangled between the teeth,
supreme sweetness,
sugar that is water, water that is sugar,
juice between threads,
small planet between red and yellow,
fruit that comes away secreting gum,
yellow fruit blushing
excusing itself for its own perfection.
The mango is proof
of the existence of God.

IV

1

Las aves duermen mientras vuelan.
Para volar es necesario un abandono
sólo posible en el sueño.
Notas que no pertenecen a la vigilia,
que vienen del mundo de los que duermen,
notas soñadas por un colibrí cuando vuela.

2

Aleteo para permanecer en el mismo punto,
quieto entre el aire quieto,
inmune a la gravedad,
colibrí casi flor, bálsamo al ojo.

3

Huellas
como la huella el ala de un pájaro deja en el aire.
Susurro que apenas se ve como el gesto mudo de una boca.
Visiones que son revelación de la tiniebla pura.
Nada tangible en este paisaje,
tacto que tantea y no toca.

PIECES FOR PIANO

IV

1

Birds sleep on the wing.
To fly one needs an abandon
only possible in sleep.
Notes that do not belong to wakefulness,
that come from the world of those who sleep,
notes sounded by a hummingbird as it flies.

2

Wingbeat to remain in the same spot,
still amid the still air,
immune to gravity,
hummingbird almost flower, balm to the eye.

3

Traces
like the trace a bird's wing leaves on the air.
A rustling scarcely visible like a mouth's mute motion.
Visions that reveal utter darkness.
Nothing tangible in this landscape,
touch that seeks its way and does not touch.

VII

1

Si la lluvia cantara
sonaría como este piano lento
que da vueltas en torno a un solo motivo.
Pero la lluvia no canta.
La lluvia es silencio desde el piso doce.
Y sólo percute contra el vidrio cuando el viento la empuja
y ella suena susurrante o brusca.
Casi siempre la lluvia pasa en silencio frente a mi ventana
y yo intuyo que lleva ganas de cantar un canto triste,
un canto de piano sin palabras posibles.

2

Yo no soy.
Soy las cosas que pasan,
la lluvia bendita.
Si algo soy, soy alguien que ve llover,
que oye llover,
soy un oído entre la música del viento,
una piel entre el frío del viento,
alguien que yace
mientras afuera hay una ciudad que no conozco,
que apenas olfateo.
Soy ese perfume que desconocía.

VII

I

If the rain could sing
it would sound like this slow piano
that plays variations on a single theme.
But the rain doesn't sing.
The rain is silent on the twelfth floor.
And it only taps against the pane when the wind drives it there
and then it sounds sharp or else murmurs.
Almost always the rain passes before my window in silence
and I sense it would like to sing a sad song,
a song for piano without possible words.

2

I am not me.
I am the things that pass by,
the blessed rain.
If I am anything, I am someone who watches the rain,
who hears the rain,
I am an ear within the music of the wind,
a skin within the cold of the wind,
someone who lies down
while outside there is a city I do not know,
that I barely smell.
I am that scent I didn't recognize.

3

Apunto palabras que acomodo entre dos notas.
Soy un bálsamo.
Palabras como alondra o jacaranda
que vuelan o florecen entre mi libreta.
Las letras de mi jacaranda son negras,
pero la palabra tiene el color de la jacaranda florecida.
Las letras de mi alondra están quietas,
pero la palabra alondra vibra
como el cuerpo vivo de la alondra,
como su canto vibra.

3

I write down words that I fit between two notes.
I am a balm.
Words like *alondra* or *jacaranda*,
that fly or flower inside my notebook.
The letters of my jacaranda are black,
but the word has the colour of a flowering jacaranda.
The letters of my *alondra*, my lark, are still,
but the word quivers
like the living body of the lark,
like its quivering song.

I

Música de sábado por la tarde, canciones desajándose, sonidos de
   carbono catorce, piano fantasma resucitando en el silencio,
amnesia que cura una guitarra, espectros que regresan bailando,
   música que suena medio siglo más tarde.
Aún es sábado de día y yo *quiero escaparme con la vieja luna,*
   quiero revivir la noche porque la vieja luna volverá.
Ya se sabe que el tiempo no importa, que no hay recuerdo viejo,
   que ni el olvido vale.
En la tarde de sábado una canción rompe el silencio y entonces
   la memoria inventa otro silencio más denso, un silencio azul
   sin sobresaltos. Esa música refunde los tiempos del verbo,
   unifica los más antiguos días con este mismo instante.
Flor eterna como ninguna flor.
No hay pasado con este canto, los recuerdos no son recuerdos,
   son respiración, destello, instante.
El olvido, entonces, es un filtro, el refinamiento, la destilación de
   la música. *Niebla del riachuelo, amarrado al recuerdo, yo sigo*
   esperando, niebla de riachuelo, de ese amor por siempre me
   vas alejando. Nunca más su voz nombró mi nombre junto a mí,
   esa voz que dijo adiós.
No, no se disfraza de oscuridad la tarde, actúa a plena luz, muestra
   a plena luz su magia sin trucos, su transparencia que me vence.
La tarde está hecha de silencio, de la voluntad de suprimir todo
   sonido, la tarde de sábado es solo luz, una luz indiferente al
   asombro, la luz única se esta ciudad que es mía, donde el
   viento tampoco suena pero sabe enfriar las cosas.

THE BODY AND ANOTHER THING

I

Music of Saturday afternoon, songs unwaning, sounds of Carbon-14,
   phantom piano coming to life in the silence,
amnesia cured by a guitar, ghosts that return dancing, music heard
   a half century later.
It's still day-time on a Saturday and I *want to escape with the old moon,*
   I want to relive the night because the old moon will return.
Everybody knows that time doesn't matter, that there is no such thing as an old
   memory, that oblivion is uncertain.
On Saturday afternoon a song breaks the silence and then memory
   creates another, denser silence, a blue silence, no shocks. That music
   merges the tenses of the verb, joins the most distant days with
   this very moment.
Eternal flower like no other flower.
There is no past with this singing, memories are not memories, they are breath,
   sparkle, instant.
Oblivion, then, is a filter, the refinement, the distillation of music.
   Niebla del riachuelo, amarrado al recuerdo, yo sigo
   esperando, niebla de riachuelo, de ese amor por siempre me
   vas alejando. Nunca más su voz nombró mi nombre junto a mí,
   esa voz que dijo adiós.[1]
No, the evening does not dress up in darkness, it plays out all lit up, shows
   its guileless magic all lit up, its clarity overwhelms me.
The afternoon is made of silence, of the will to block out all sound, Saturday
   afternoon is only light, a light indifferent to surprise, the light unique to this
   city, which is mine, where the wind makes no sound but knows how to chill
   things.

Quedan el calor del alma, el tiempo detenido, ningún recuerdo, todo en presente, y una euforia que me llevará hasta el fin.

The heat of the soul remains, time stopped still, no memories, everything in the present, and a euphoria that will take me to the end.

The words are taken from a famous 1937 Tango performed by Edmundo Rivero, which translates roughly as: *Mist from the stream, tied to memory, I am still waiting, mist from the stream, that love forever walking away from me. Her voice will never say my name again, at my side, that voice that said goodbye.*

4

Dolores en la pierna, picadas que me estremecen, dolores que pastilla
   no borra, sólo amengua.
Cambio de piel, metamorfosis, necesidad de aislarse a esperar la epifanía
   o el parto.
Necesidad de recogimiento, necesidad de desconectar los sentidos,
   necesidad de estar aislado, de cerrar las cortinas, de eliminar todo ruido.
Cero fachada y noche, cero derroche.
Mudo de piel y una parte dentro de mí hace crac o algo parecido.
Intuyo otra manera de llevar el tiempo.
Indiferente al ruido, ausente del ruido, atento a las premoniciones,
   a ciertos dichosos augurios, al vacío.

5

Hay noches que son de violín, otras de piano y otras que se deslizan
   en silencio o entre el tamborileo de la lluvia en los techos.
Noches que retornan a otras noches olvidadas cabalgando sobre
   viejas canciones.
Los domingos, cuando comienza el insomnio, aparecen antiguos
   estribillos,
perdona mi franqueza que tal vez juzgues descaro,
si yo encontrara un alma como la mía,
y un vaho de anís me transporta a una oscuridad de otros años, a
   una ebriedad distinta,
cuando tenía la certeza de que una revelación estaba cerca
y ninguna herida me había dejado cicatrices.

4

Pains in the leg, stinging that make me shudder, pains that pills do not erase,
  only diminish.
Change of skin, metamorphosis, the need to isolate myself and await
  epiphany or birth.
The need for withdrawal, for disconnecting the senses, the need to be isolated,
  to shut the curtains, to block out all noise.
No pretence, no nightlife, no excess.
A shedding of skin and a part of me snaps, or something similar.
I sense another way of spending my time.
Immune to the noise, absent from the noise, alert to premonitions,
  to certain happy omens, to the emptiness.

5

There are violin nights, and piano nights and other nights that slide by
  in silence or between the drumming of rain on rooftops.
Nights that revisit other, forgotten nights, riding on old songs.
On Sundays, when the insomnia begins, ancient refrains surface:
forgive my frankness which you may find impertinent,
but I might have found a soul like my own,
a whiff of anise lifts me towards the darkness of another time,
  a different intoxication,
when I was certain that a revelation was near
and no wound had left me scarred.

7

Yo soy mi cuerpo, me dicen. Lo otro que me habita no soy yo y
no llevará mi nombre cuando muera, será parte de un todo
sin memoria y yo no seré ni la sombre de lo que fue mi alma.
Yo moriré, yo moriré como carne y como yo, pobre y efímero
animal, bestia gozosa, y esa otra cosa que es el alma, seguirá
sin recordarme más.
Mi fantasma no dirá que fui yo porque yo estaré más allá de sus
recuerdos. El cuerpo de mis gozos se extinguirá entre la tierra,
será ceniza, y lo otro que estuvo dentro de mí será aliento de
otro ser, será parte de otra nada.

11

El cuerpo está hecho de tiempo, tiempo inexorable, absurdamente simple,
tiempo que no entiendo, tiempo curvo, tiempo hueco, ahora mismo hueco.
Tiempo con pasado y con mañana y con un hueco, tiempo con nada, tiempo
sin hoy, en mis narices el hueco del presente capaz de no existir y de ser
mi única existencia.
Eso es el cuerpo, el cuerpo hecho de tiempo.
El cuerpo y esa otra cosa y esa otra.
El cuerpo y el alma y esa otra.
El cuerpo y el alma y la muerte.
La muerte que es cuando el tiempo ha dejado de pasarnos.
El tiempo, que es el cuerpo.

7

I am my body, they say. The other who lives in me is not I and
   will not bear my name when it dies, it will be part of a whole
   without memory and I will not even be the shadow of what
   was my soul. I will die, and I will die like flesh and like me,
   poor and ephemeral animal, joyful beast, and that other thing
   which is the soul, will follow on without remembering any more.
My ghost will not say that it was me because I will be beyond
   its memories. The body of my pleasures will be erased beneath
   the earth, will be ashes, and the other that was inside me will be
   another being's breath, will be part of another nothing.

11

The body is made of time, inexorable time, absurdly simple, time
   that I don't understand, curved time, empty time, empty at this moment.
Time with a past and a future and an emptiness, time with nothing, time
   without today, in my nostrils the emptiness of the present capable of not
   existing and of being my unique existence.
That is the body, the body made of time.
The body and that other thing and that other.
The body and the soul and that other thing.
The body and the soul and death.
Death which is when time has stopped happening to us.
Time, which is the body.

22

Las palabras no son las cosas pero las palabras son la cosa.
Las palabras no son las cosas pero cambian las cosas, a veces
    cambian las cosas.
Las palabras son sólo palabras, pero las cosas son algo más que
    las cosas.
Las cosas no son palabras pero las palabras son cosas.
Las cosas son cosas o son palabras pero las palabras son sólo palabras.
Y son la cosa.

24

Infidencias de otro tiempo, santos lugares de la melancolía,
    química para mirarme en un espejo y localizar el sitio de la
    herida atávica.
La víspera del viaje, antes del vuelo, me sé la marca de la especie
    y me siento más liviano: aquí la cicatriz, exactamente aquí,
    pero soy otro distinto de aquél que recibió la herida.
La música del violín huele a jazmines y el piano suena como si
    fuera un líquido sin prisa y yo atravieso otro umbral y siento
    el aire de una madrugada distinta en los pulmones.

22

Words are not things but words are the thing.
Words are not things but they change things, sometimes
    things change.
Words are only words, but things are somewhat more than
    things.
Things are not words but words are things.
Things are things or are words but words are only words.
And they are the thing.

24

Betrayals of another time, holy places of melancholy,
    chemistry to look at myself in a mirror and pinpoint
    the location of the atavistic wound.
The eve of the journey, before the flight, I know the mark of the species
    and I feel lighter: here is the scar, precisely here,
    but I am different altogether from the one who received the wound.
The violin music smells of jasmine and the piano sounds as if it were
    an unhurried liquid and I cross another threshold and feel the air
    of a different dawn in my lungs.

28

Aquí tu piel,
su tacto en mi memoria nublándome la vista,
tu piel, cortina que me separa del mundo,
que me distrae de todo lo que me distrae,
tu piel que es humo,
irrealidad donde habito.

34

Ardua tarea fumigar las ansias, desprenderse de los nudos invisibles;
    reposar sin calor ni sopor, no mirar el sitio donde arden con
    despacio las espinas: hace ya mucho se borraron las señales
    del camino de púas.
El olvido es también útil: no soy sólo recuerdos, soy una larga y ya
    borrada lista de olvidos.

35

No espero al otro que también soy yo.
Mi doble no es el huésped: es probable que quien viene sea el original
    y yo la copia.
Tal vez solamente un borrador.

2 8

Here is your skin,
the memory of its touch clouding my vision,
your skin, a curtain that shields me from the world,
that distracts me from all that distracts me,
your skin which is smoke,
unreality where I dwell.

3 4

An arduous task fumigating desires, untying the invisible knots,
   resting without heat or stupor, not watching the place where
   the needles burn slowly: long ago now that the signposts for the way
   of thorns were wiped clean.
Forgetting is also useful: I am not only memories, I am a long and already
   erased list of forgotten things.

3 5

I am not waiting for the other who is also me.
My double is not the host: it is likely that the one coming is the original
   and I the copy.
Maybe only a draft.

LOS AMIGOS MUERTOS

Si ahora regresaran llegarían con su edad intacta,
más allá de la muerte, inmortales
con aire de ignorar lo nuevo que hay en el mundo,
sin interés en nada distinto de indagar lo que ahora soy.
¿Por qué las canas y la panza?
¿Por qué mi trajinado traje mortal que cruje tanto y mi cojera?
¿Por qué mi apatía con el mundo, mi apatía conmigo, mi desgano?
¿Por qué mi fastidio con el ruido y sus ruindades?
¿Por qué mi amor al silencio, mi mutismo?
También preguntarían perversos por qué conmigo la muerte es indolente.
Si ahora regresaran, llegarían dándome un abrazo que todavía extraño.

DEAD FRIENDS

If they returned now they would come with their age unchanged,
from the other side of death, immortal,
unaware of what was new in the world,
without interest in anything more than finding out what I have now become.
Why the grey hair and the paunch?
Why my exhausted mortal attire that creaks so – and my limp?
Why my apathy with the world, my apathy with myself, my indifference?
Why my exasperation with noise and all its meanness?
Why my love for silence, my lack of words.
They would also ask, perversely, why death has been idle with me.
If now they returned, they would come with an embrace that I still crave.

I 2

Me dijo,
varias veces me dijo:
– no tratas de entender el tiempo, no te pongas a seguir lo que se alarga, mirar
   el reloj prolonga las esperas, tú lo sabes.
Olvídate del tiempo, no lo expliques porque mentirás, no lo entiendas porque
   entonces estarás loco,
no te metas con el tiempo – me advirtió como si el tiempo fuera el árbol
   prohibido del paraíso,
– por tu bien te lo digo: deja el tiempo quieto, no te metas, no te metas – repetía
   y repetía.
– De ser posible no cargues reloj, más bien aprende a adivinar la hora,
   me dijo y sonreía. Nunca vi la sonrisa de Dios, pero es fácil saber cuándo
   acompaña sus palabras con sonrisas.
Todo eso me dijo Dios: el tiempo es uno los temas favoritos de Dios.
Le pregunté algún día:
– Si quieres que me olvide de explicar el tiempo, ¿porqué, entonces, me hablas
   tanto del tiempo?
Me contestó sentencioso: – El tiempo es el secreto del plato, el ingrediente que
   nunca conocerá nadie.
Me atreví con un Dios ensimismado en el misterio:
– Hablas como si tú mismo no te atrevieras con el tiempo.
Son muy grandes los silencios de Dios, y aquel día sentí la gravedad de su
   silencio. Como un viento helado me caló su silencio.
Al rato Dios, que por algo es Dios, dejó oír una risita maliciosa y me dijo:
– Tú conoces la eternidad desde afuera. Así, del mismo modo, conozco yo el
   tiempo, desde fuera de él.
Ahora lo pienso: Dios es paciente porque no espera. Dios no conoce la espera,
   no sabe de las ansias, ignora el mal y desconoce el tiempo.

1 2

He told me,
several times He told me
– don't try to understand time, don't go chasing what only drags on and on,
　　watching the clock prolongs the wait, as you know.
Forget about time, don't explain it because you will lie, don't understand it
　　because then you will go mad,
don't meddle with time, He warned me as if time were the forbidden tree of paradise,
– I'm telling you for your own good: leave time alone, don't meddle with it, don't
　　meddle with it – He said again and again.
– If at all possible do not wind your clock, better that you learn to guess the hour,
　　He told me and He smiled. I have never seen the smile of God, but it is easy
　　to tell when His words are accompanied by smiles.
All of this God told me: time is one of God's favourite topics.
One day I asked Him:
– if you want me to forget about explaining time, why then do you talk to me so
　　much about time?
He answered me sententiously: – time is the secret of the recipe, the ingredient
　　that nobody will ever know.
I was bold with this God absorbed in mystery:
– you speak as if you yourself were wary of time.
Very great are the silences of God, and that day I felt the gravity of his silence.
　　Like an icy wind, his silence penetrated me.
At length God, who is not God for nothing, let out a malicious chuckle and told
　　me:
– You know eternity from the outside. In the same way, I understand time, from
　　outside of it.
Now I think this: God is patient because He does not wait. God does not
　　understand waiting, He does not know anxiety, disregards evil and is unaware
　　of time.

Venía yo en un avión desde el sur.

De la pampa a los Andes a la selva a mi meseta.

No miraba por la ventana: oía música, dormía y oía música dormido.

No pensaba en nada. Es la mejor manera de ir en un avión.

No pensaba en nada. Es la mejor manera de ir.

No miraba por la ventana: temo a la selva. Temo a ese verde monótono y oscuro, un solo tono de un solo verde que interrumpen pantanos o que los ríos cortan.

No pensaba ni miraba y de súbito Él me habló y me impulsó a mirar la espesa y repelente selva.

Me dijo:

-Cuando soy agua, soy el río Amazonas.

Sólo eso me dijo y lo entendí contemplando el Amazonas a treinta mil pies de altura a velocidad de crucero.

Lo entendí: para que exista este río tiene Dios que convertirse en agua.

14

I was coming from the south in an aeroplane.

From the Pampa to the Andes to the jungle to my high plateau.

I didn't look out the window: I listened to music, slept and listened
    to music while I slept.

I didn't think about anything. It's the best way to travel in an aeroplane.

I didn't think about anything. It's the best way to travel.

I didn't look out the window: I'm afraid of the jungle. I'm afraid of that dark
    and monotonous green, a single tone of a single green interrupted or
    broken up by lakes or rivers.

I wasn't thinking or looking when of a sudden He spoke to me and moved me
    to look at the dense and repellent jungle.

He told me:

– When I am water, I am the River Amazon.

He said only this and I understood him, gazing at the Amazon at thirty
    thousand feet, at cruising speed.

I understood: for this river to exist God has to turn Himself to water.

IMPOSSIBLE LOVES: OF TIME AND PARADOX
An afterword

Darío Jaramillo Agudelo is one of the outstanding poets of the Spanish-speaking world. The recipient of many awards, including Colombia's National Poetry Prize (2017) and Spain's Federico García Lorca Prize (2018), he is, above all, a poet concerned with the concepts of *time* (the word makes more than fifty appearances in the poems included here) and *paradox*, as the title of this selection, taken from one of his best-known sequences, might suggest.

Jaramillo was born on 28 July, 1947, in Santa Rosa de Osos, Antioquia; a medium-sized town in Colombia's northern uplands. It is widely acknowledged that the experiences of a child before the age of seven are ingrained and irrevocable, and dreamlike motifs from early childhood recur consistently throughout Jaramillo's work. When he was seven, the family moved to the provincial capital, Medellín, where he later attended high school. Jaramillo notes of his education with the Jesuits that he was taught philosophy as though it were 'a solid building, complete in itself, unquestionable and unchangeable.' Needless to say, he claims in the same autobiographical essay, he swam in a sea of doubts against such certainty. As a bright and (in his own words) impertinent sixteen-year old, he once met and chatted with J.L Borges. A photograph exists of this meeting; the confident, handsome young Colombian sits with studied abandon alongside South America's blind and oblivious literary colossus, lending the picture a flavour of both portentousness and unreality. On being questioned by his young reader why he claimed one thing in a certain section of his work and its exact opposite in another, the Argentine maestro answered that it was clear that young Jaramillo had read his texts many more times than he, Borges, had written them. Whether or not this trickster response instilled in the aspiring poet a desire to perplex his readers with similar conundrums remains unclear, but when I questioned Jaramillo on the evident contradiction in one of his own works (Part 22 of his sequence 'El cuerpo y otra cosa' / 'The body and another thing'), in which we are told both that 'words are not things' and 'words are things') he merely shrugged, and agreed that yes, it was a contradiction, before muttering 'pero las palabras *son* la cosa' (but words *are* the thing). Only later did I find a clue to this enigmatic proposition, in an essay by Jaramillo in which he approvingly quotes from Joubert's *Pensées*: 'In ordinary language, words serve to recall things; but when language is really poetical, things always serve to recall words.'

Initially intending to become a civil engineer, Jaramillo eventually graduated in Law and Economics from the Universidad Javeriana of Bogotá, and in the years that followed, he worked in various posts as an arts administrator, which included managing the Bank of Colombia's cultural support programme and coordinating the national network of public libraries and museums. He has written, of his own working life, that he is someone who 'has always worked in different jobs, including ones opposed to poetry, such as the law, yet was never able to escape the persistent obsessions related to the art of conjuring with words.' However, the day-job inevitably brought him into contact with individuals close to the centres of power during a particularly troubled period of Colombian history.

In 1989, Jaramillo was the victim of a bomb attack that resulted in the amputation of his right leg below the knee, a loss that has become part of a gently self-deprecating personal mythology in the poems, as well – in a broader sense – as a legacy of his country's fifty-year-long civil conflict, which wreaked havoc on the land and destroyed or overturned the lives of millions of Colombians, and whose shadow, inevitably, is cast across the poet's work. Despite having suffered as a direct casualty of the war, the poet was outspoken in his support of the peace process between the government of Juan Manuel Santos and the FARC, before the national referendum in 2016.

In terms of poetic mentors, Jaramillo claims that as a young writer, he was (as were many of his contemporaries across the Spanish-speaking Americas) much influenced by the Chilean Nicanor Parra, and that Parra's work, more than that of any other poet, came to him as a revelation. One consequence of that influence was to develop a strongly narrative style, in defiance of the literary status quo in Colombia at that time, whose poetry was known for its rigid, formal and declamatory style. Other, more local influences on the young writer were his namesake, the *nadaista* Jaime Jaramillo Escobar, as well as Rogelio Echevarría and Mario Rivero. Unsurprisingly, Jaramillo's first collection, *Historias* (1974), contains poems that reflect the direct influence of Parra, including some entertaining portraits of historical figures and family members. By Jaramillo's own admission, much of the work in this collection was concerned with poetry itself, and is meta-textual and self-referential in tone. For reasons of space, therefore, I begin this selection with poems from the more developed 1978 collection, *Tratado de Retórica – o la necesidad de la poesía* ('Treatise on rhetoric – or the necessity of poetry').

'Razones del ausente / Reasons for his absence' is the poem that introduces Jaramillo's own selected poems, in the edition published in Mexico by Era (2014), and I have retained it in opening position in the current selection. Other poems from that 1978 collection include 'El oficio / The Trade', 'Penúltima biografía imaginaria' / 'Penultimate Imaginary Biography', 'Otra *ars poética una: El tiempo*' / 'Another *ars poetica* 1: Time', 'Relato' / 'Story' and 'Venganza' / 'Vengeance'. The ordering of the poems follows on chronologically; next comes 'Poemas de Amor' / 'Love Poems' (1986), a collection which has received extraordinary critical and popular acclaim around Latin America, its opening poem winning a contest on Colombian national TV with over 20,000 votes, for the 'greatest love poem' in February 1989. Also published in 1986 were 'Álbum de fotos' / 'Photograph Album', the 'Nostalgia' sequence, 'Job otra vez' / 'Job again', 'Testimonio acerca del hermano' / 'Testimony concerning my brother' and 'Platón borracho' / 'Plato drunk'. 'Cuando decimos piedra' / 'When we say stone' is from 1995, while the titular 'Amores impossibles' / 'Impossible loves' appeared in 2001, as did 'Desollaminetos' / 'Flayings' and 'Mozart en la autopista' / 'Mozart on the Motorway'. The 'Gatos' / 'Cats' sequence was originally published as a collection in 2006, the year that also saw the publication of 'Caucho' / 'Rubber Tree' and 'Sabor' / 'Taste' in the collection *La voz interior*. 'Piezas para piano' / 'Pieces for Piano' appeared in 2008, in *Cuadernos de música*. 'El cuerpo y otra cosa' / 'The Body and another thing' was published in 2016, winning Colombia's national prize for poetry the following year. The two poems from 'Conversaciones con Dios' / 'Conversations with God' are taken from a new 40-poem sequence of that title, currently unpublished in Spanish.

As I have already suggested, some of the poetry is flecked with images from the poet's childhood in rural Antioquia. The appearance of a hummingbird in his bedroom, aged five, which appears in 'Nostalgia 1' and his initial terror and subsequent fascination, has remained, for Jaramillo, a fundamental image. He claims to have undergone a kind of epiphany with this experience, which led to an awareness of transience and of perfect, unrepeatable beauty – but also of shock, amazement and fear, at being in the world of creatures, and a burgeoning sense of mortality. He also recalls excursions to collect wild flowers with his mother as fomenting a close affinity with the local habitat. When discussing these early years, in person as well as in the poems, Darío sometimes gives the impression of his childhood as having been a protracted and astonishing hallucination.

It should be pointed out that Jaramillo is also a highly acclaimed novelist, and that, as Enrique Salas-Durazo has observed, many of the themes that appear in Jaramillo's poems – lost love, friendship, the 'doubling' or 'masking' of the self – re-surface in the fiction. This dual identity, as poet and novelist, is sometimes regarded with suspicion, especially in the English-speaking world, where it is assumed that a writer cannot (or should not) excel at both genres. Yet no one, as José Emilio Pacheco has noted, questions whether Goethe or Victor Hugo was primarily a poet or novelist. Jaramillo has written of his own position in an essay on the creative process: 'I have to confess that I don't properly understand the difference between literary genres', and goes on approvingly to cite Virginia Woolf, who declared the only literary genre to be poetry. His point is taken up by the Mexican essayist Sergio Pitol, who says that for Jaramillo, all notable experience is poetry, and all writing derives from – or, I would suggest, is a *translation* of – that initial poetic assimilation or formulation. However, apart from the rather obvious distinction that can be made between the narrative poems and (shorter) love poems, Jaramillo says he never really thinks in terms of a 'poetic' theory or *Ars poetica* (despite, paradoxically, the existence of at least two poems with this title in his oeuvre) but thinks of his poems, rather, as 'experiments'. In interviews, he displays a consistent reluctance to explain his poetry, preferring to claim ignorance about deeper themes or unifying motifs, a reluctance which, however, he goes to some lengths to overcome in his own essays on the creative process, notably *Historia de una pasión* (2006) and assorted talks delivered at conferences and literary festivals under the title 'Lo que me hizo escritor'.

In *Historia de una pasión*, however, he does set out a credo of his own writing practice:

> I write because I am entranced by words, because by writing I cross other thresholds, because it is a quiet pursuit, because it is a meticulous pursuit, because I enjoy correcting, finding words, rhythmic solutions, I write because I adore silence, because I like being alone, because I can exit from time, because inventing stories allows me to unfold in a fascinating way that I don't know how to explain ... I write for pure pleasure ... I write to complete myself, to take myself out of the day and into a notebook, into a world of words that want to be more than words. (pp. 73-4).

The word that I have translated here as 'unfold' (desdoblar) has an alternative meaning, which is to 'double oneself' or split in two. His poetic world – often centred on an interrogation of memory, love, and loss – is infused throughout with a sense of duality; not merely the duality of the divided self, but of the individual as one possible version of multiple selves. Jaramillo's frequently iterated 'doubling' of the self is most evident in reference to his 'brothers', those beings that at times are his companions, and yet at others, and equally convincingly, projections of the self as 'other'. Darío is an only child, and these 'brothers' of his are often chaotic, wild characters, given to Dionysian excess, addicted to drink or drugs. More than one of them commits suicide. I used to get the feeling – especially when translating the long, relatively early poem, 'Testimonio acerca del hermano' / 'Testimony concerning my brother' – that Darío was writing about himself when he wrote of this particular brother, and it is true, in this poem, that identity shifts between the poem's narrator and his brother ('we both know that the two of us, loners, will never be apart'). This *other* is always around somewhere, observing, hiding in the alcoves or behind the curtains, a Borgesian double who somehow knows more than the original Darío. In fact, in the closing poem of 'El cuerpo y otra cosa' / 'The Body and another thing' (no. 35) the poet suspects his double is the real version, and he, the poet, merely a draft (*un borrador*): 'I am not waiting for the other who is also me. / My double is not the host: it is likely that the one coming is the original and I the copy. / Maybe only a draft.'

This doubling has other resonances in our reading of the poetry: it ties in with Jaramillo's confident assertion, in one of our conversations, that, to adopt Galen Strawson's paradigm, he regards himself as an 'episodic' individual (one who is essentially 'a different person' at distinct stages of his life) rather than one persuaded by any sense of narrative continuity, the possessor of a single, essential identity. It is paradoxical, therefore, to encounter in these pages a pervasive sense of longing (including for things that have not happened, as in the 'Impossible Loves' poems), and yearning for the state of wonder described in the 'Nostalgia' poems. He says he doesn't dwell in the past – but he writes poems about nostalgia and dead loves. He writes about music as though it were a striving toward the ideal state of silence. He writes a book about cats and says he prefers dogs. Again and again we encounter the deep sense of paradox at the heart of Jaramillo's writing. But perhaps this reliance on paradox is, ultimately, an ability to live with contradictions, or at least with uncertainty – the expression of which is at the heart of his poetry.

Jaramillo is also, as already indicated, a poet concerned with time. The concept of time recurs in his poems again and again, frequently – in full Shakespearean mode – interlaced with meditations on decrement and death, and in particular, the deaths of friends or 'brothers'. The early statement of poetic intent, ironically titled 'Another *Ars poetica* 1' (and in which the reader might detect more than a trace of Dylan Thomas) is entirely concerned with time, opening with the lines: 'Of the geometry of time this poem that runs over / the cold skin of minutes that neither wait nor pester, / of the line of days sown in the metallic light of the dead, / forced to flower by such life as flows in their water-clock veins'. His poem, Jaramillo claims, is 'peering sideways at death', and yet is 'impotent' before time's ruthlessness.

Other time-obsessed poems refer to religious themes, as well as artfully drawing on ideas from quantum theory. In 'El cuerpo y otra cosa' / The body and another thing', we are reminded that time is embedded – or embodied – in ourselves: 'The body is made of time, inexorable time, absurdly simple, time / that I don't understand, curved time, empty time, empty at this moment.' Death, which we might normally conceive of as the end of 'our time' is re-framed by Jaramillo as 'when time stops happening to us' ('cuando el tiempo ha dejado de pasarnos'). However, all attempts to understand time are doomed to failure, since, as we learn in 'Conversations with God', even the deity does not stop worrying about it. In poem 11 of the sequence, the human questioner puts it to God: 'If you want me to forget about explaining time, why then do you talk to me so much about time?' God's answer does not satisfy the poem's narrator, who tells God: 'you speak as if you yourself were wary of time.' It becomes apparent that the All-knowing, All-powerful cannot answer any of his interlocutor's questions because he doesn't have the slightest idea how to. He is patient 'because He does not wait' and therefore 'does not understand waiting'. His omnipotence (and supposed benevolence) is qualified by the fact that he 'disregards evil and is unaware of time' ('ignora el mal y desconoce el tiempo').

Jaramillo claims in one of his essays that, following the success of his hugely popular 'Poemas de amor' / 'Love poems', he decided to publish a kind of 'antidote', with the title 'Impossible Loves' in order to explore the emotions and advantages of loves that do not (or cannot) exist. The decision to name this book after that sequence seemed to take itself: poetry is not 'merely' the celebration of truth and beauty, as Keats, another of Jaramillo's mentors, might have put it, but also the examination of the mundane, the absurd, the paradoxical and the impossible. All of it swimming in an impossible sea of time, 'which is the body . . . and that other thing, and that other.'

REFERENCES

Jaramillo Agudelo, Darío, *Historia de una pasión* (2006) Valencia: Pre-Textos.

Jaramillo Agudelo, Darío, *Lo que me hizo escritor* (2018): Three essays (unpublished, personal correspondence).

Joubert, Joseph, *Pensées*, (1896) translated by Henry Attwell. https://archive.org/details/pensesjoubert00joubgoog/page/n126

Pacheco, José Emilio (2003) 'Nota al pie de un libro de poemas', in Jaramillo Agudelo, Darío, *Libros de Poemas*, Bogotá: Fondo de Cultura Económica.

Pitol, Sergio (2003) 'El té de las cinco y la poesía', in Jaramillo Agudelo, Darío, *Libros de Poemas*, Bogotá: Fondo de Cultura Económica.

Salas-Durazo, Enrique (2016) 'The intersections between poetry and fiction in two Colombian writers of the twentieth century: Álvaro Mutis and Darío Jaramillo Agudelo.' In Raymond Leslie Williams (ed.) *A History of Colombian* Literature, New York: Cambridge University Press.

Strawson, Galen (2004) 'Against Narrativity' in *Ratio (new series)* XVII 4 December 2004, pp 428-452.

ACKNOWLEDGEMENTS

Darío Jaramillo has always insisted that he wanted the selection of poems to be mine, and although we have met several times to discuss these translations, he has never once indicated which poems he would prefer to be included and which to omit. During these meeting with the poet – always conducted, on Darío's part, with extraordinary courtesy and patience – I was able to resolve many of my questions, especially those regarding the idiosyncrasies of Colombian Spanish. From a translator's perspective, the benefits of working closely with the author are indisputable. In so far as any translation can reproduce the music – or the weather – of the language in which they were composed, I have opted for loyalty to the source text rather than inventive re-interpretation. Any failure to capture the sense or quality of the original is entirely my own.

I would like to thank the Arts Council of Wales for a Creative Wales award in 2014, which allowed me to travel to Colombia and spend time with several poets in that remarkable country. The translations also benefitted from the award of a three-week residency at the Banff Centre for the Arts, Alberta, in the Canadian Rockies during June 2018. Many thanks, therefore, to the Banff Centre, and the programme director for literary translation, Pedro Serrano, for helping this project come to fruition. I would also like to extend enormous gratitude to my brilliant friend, Inés Garland, who provided unflagging support and copious criticism of these translations over the course of numerous emails, responding promptly and politely to my often repetitive and obsessive questions. Finally, my thanks are due to Michael Schmidt of Carcanet Press, who has embraced this project from the outset.